Decodable Reader

Unit 1

Mc
Graw
Hill

Contents

by Magali Rivera

We Can! I

by Allison Rivera
illustrated by Eva Vagreti

Jan Can Pack 9
Short *a*

Sit Down Kids! 17

Short *i*

A Big Plan 25

l-blends

Is Rock Fun? 33

Short *o*

We Can!

by Magali Rivera

We can go to  .

school

We can  .

paint

We can  .

read

We can play.

We can .

eat

We can!

Jan Can Pack

by Allison Rivera
illustrated by Eva Vagreti

Jan packs.

Jan has a cap.

What can Jan pack?

Jan packs a bag.

Jan packs a pad.

Jan packs for **school**!
Dad **does** **not**.

Sit Down Kids!

by Emily Hansen
illustrated by Kate Flanagan

Sid sits.

Liz sits. Tim sits.

Kids go quick!

Sid sits **down**.
Liz sits down.

Sid is **up**.

Liz is up. Quick!

Will Sid sit?

Will Liz sit?

Liz is **out**.

Sid is **very** quick.

A Big Plan

by John Niles
illustrated by Olivia Cole

Jill has a big plan.

Jill will **pull** a sack down.

Jill will clip, clip rag bits.

A flag will **be** **good**.

Jill clips and slips rag bits.

Come, see a big pig flag!

Is Rock Fun?

by Harold Kurtz
illustrated by Lynne Avril

Bam, bam, bam.
Bob can **make** rock.

Rat-a-tat.

Bob taps on.

They do not like rock.

Dad has a big box.
Mom is glad.

Mom has a box, **too**.
Dad is glad.

They can block it.
Rock is **fun**!

Unit 1

Week 1 • *We Can!* .... **page 1**
Word Count: 17

High-Frequency Words
Review: *can, go, play, to, we*

Week 2 • *Jan Can Pack* ....**page 9**
Word Count: 30

Decodable Words
Target Phonics Element: Short *a*
bag, can, cap, Dad, has, Jan, pack, packs, pad

High-Frequency Words
does, not, school, what
Review: *for*

Week 3 • *Sit Down Kids!* .... **page 17**
Word Count: 38

Decodable Words
Target Phonics Element: Short *i*
is, kids, Liz, quick, Sid, sit, sits, Tim, will

High-Frequency Words
down, out, up, very
Review: *go*

Week 4 • *A Big Plan* .... page 25

Word Count: 37

Decodable Words

Target Phonics Element: *l*-blends
clip, clips, flag, plan, slips
Review: *big, bits, has, Jill, pig, rag, sack, will*

High-Frequency Words
be, come, good, pull
Review: *and, down, see*

Week 5 • *Is Rock Fun?* ....page 33

Word Count: 44

Decodable Words

Target Phonics Element: Short *o*
block, Bob, box, Mom, on, rock
Review: *bam, big, can, Dad, glad, has, is,*
not, rat-a-tat, taps

High-Frequency Words
fun, make, they, too
Review: *do, like*

Decoding skills taught to date:

Phonics: Short *a;* Short *i;* *l*-Blends; Short *o*

Structural Analysis: Inflectional Ending -*s* (plurals, verbs); Double Final Consonants; Alphabetical Order